CALLAWAY GARDENS
THE UNENDING SEASON

Published by
LONGSTREET PRESS, INC.
2150 Newmarket Parkway
Suite 102
Marietta, Georgia 30067

Foreword copyright © 1989 by Celestine Sibley
Photographs copyright © 1989 by James Valentine

Printed in the United States of America

1st printing, 1989

Library of Congress Catalog Number 88-083079

ISBN 0-929264-14-2

This book was printed by Arcata Graphics Kingsport Press,
in Kingsport, Tennessee. The text type was set in
Palatino by Typo-Repro Service, Inc., Atlanta, Georgia.
Design by Paulette Lambert.

Handmade art prints are available from:
Valentine Visions, a division of Russell Image Processing, Inc.
667 11th Street, NW, Suite 3, Atlanta, Georgia 30318.

CALLAWAY GARDENS
THE UNENDING SEASON

Photographs by James P. Valentine

Foreword by Celestine Sibley

LONGSTREET PRESS
ATLANTA, GEORGIA

A place with soul . . . a place where people can get away from the pressures of modern life, away from stressful existences, to retreat to a clean, natural, positive environment . . . where they can get close to nature, reach out and touch it. And when they leave they will be better people. They will be regenerated with a new spirit.

F O R E W O R D

Cason Callaway, the textile magnate, may not have had that dream, that beneficent purpose when he walked over the cottoned-out acres adjoining his country place in southwest Georgia half a century ago. He was simply taking a walk.

But a strange, almost mystical thing happened to him.

The land he trudged over was depressing, at one with the big depression of the 1930s which had sent small farmers, unable to sustain life on their famished acres, to cities. Briars and weeds and spindly trees had taken over. The soil, gashed by erosion, ran red with the bright blood of Georgia clay, and little creeks sluggishly carried off the topsoil.

Mr. Callaway was profoundly saddened.

An outdoor man who had long drawn strength and spiritual and emotional sustenance from the earth and growing things, he was disappointed and dejected by what he saw in the sunbaked land.

He could have sighed and turned back, but there was something that held him. In that near-wasteland with its tangle of briars and weeds there was suddenly a spot of color! Drawing near, Mr. Callaway saw it was a small shrub with blooms that by all his reasoning and experience he knew had no business being there on that hot summer day. The small brittle branches of the plant were those of the wild azalea. The flowers . . . they reminded him of the fragrance and sheer translucence of the roses he associated with spring's beauty! But wild azaleas did not bloom in summer.

Mystified, Mr. Callaway picked a bloom and took it home to his wife.

Loren Eisley, the famed naturalist, exploring the mysteries of man and nature, wrote: "Flowers changed the face of the planet. Without them the world we know, even man himself, would never have existed."

The flower Cason Callaway picked that day was to change the face of vast Georgia acres. Mrs. Callaway searched her books and found that it was the beautiful and rarest member of the rhododendron family — *Rhododendron prunifolium*, or plumleaf azalea, not found anywhere in the world except in a restricted area in southwest Georgia and southeast Alabama.

That was the beginning, said Howard "Bo" Callaway, Cason's son, of the gardens.

From that point on Cason Callaway was to pour energy, imagination and money into transforming depleted and dejected acres into a place not only of exceptional visual beauty but also for the ease and refreshment of the spirit and the soul. He himself knew from a life crowded with hard work and pressures that there was strength and comfort and even a fresh outlook to be gained from being in touch with nature's quiet rhythms, with the green-growing earth and its beauties. He wanted weary and discouraged men and women and their families to find relief from hard labor and society's manic distractions.

It wasn't an instantaneous decision. For a short time as he acquired twenty-five hundred acres for a garden and an additional thirty thousand to surround it, he thought of the pleasure of sharing it with many of his old friends in the business world. He and Mrs. Callaway created a new home for themselves, a log house beside a crystal stream called Blue Springs. It was natural that he, the most hospitable of men, would enjoy sharing this delightful retreat with old friends.

And, of course, his project drew the wealthy and the distinguished. Louis Bromfield, the novelist-conservationist of famed Malabar Farms, came to visit and to see how Mr. Callaway was restoring life to the soil with composting, mulching, and fertilizing. The Callaways' neighbor and close friend, President Franklin D. Roosevelt, came from his vacation cottage at Warm Springs, twenty miles away, to see what was going on. The dammed lakes stocked with fish would offer prime diversion for his fishing friends and the verandah of the big lodge he built would be a good spot for bridge players.

Then one day Mr. Callaway heard that there were intruders in the woods and went out to investigate. A family had spread a picnic lunch by one of his new lakes.

"What can I do for you, sir?" he asked the man frostily, implying that they were trespassing.

"Well," said the man, unruffled, "you might get us some crackers for the baby."

Chastened, Mr. Callaway went back to his house and got some cookies. He began to have second thoughts about the purpose of his great project. A retired chairman of the board of U.S. Steel or Shell Oil, as his son later pointed out, could "go anywhere in the world to find beauty and relaxation. But a hardware clerk in Griffin, a shoe salesman in La Grange, a factory worker in Atlanta had no place he could go and take his family for a happy weekend in beautiful surroundings or for a quiet vacation."

The dream of a garden, although new to Cason Callaway, is one of man's oldest dreams. When Callaway stood by a stream, which surprisingly ran fast and clear from the side of Pine Mountain, he was one with ancient Mesopotamians, who five thousand years before the birth of Christ paused in a valley between the Nile and the Euphrates rivers and dreamed of and planted the first garden on record.

They called it a "pleasure" garden because its purpose was not to be utilitarian but to afford beauty. Maybe, as they planned their pyramids and terraces and laid walks between blooming beds and flowering shrubs, they knew that beauty, too, has its uses.

Cason Callaway expanded this ancient concept of the pleasure garden and made it more rewarding still. To a businessman, a garden that produced vegetables for the table and to sell, that restored the famished earth, and advanced his home state's ailing economy would be the most pleasurable garden of all.

Mr. Callaway had always taken pleasure in making money. As a young man, he had entered the textile business founded by his father. His verve and enthusiasm were such that when his turn came to take over management he was able to open nine new mills, among them the world's largest rug mill. He planned to bring the same attitude and skills to his newest dream.

Pleasure garden? Of course it would be a pleasure garden, but in Cason Callaway's expanded sense of that term. Bringing back to fruitful production the soil that had been effectively killed and left as worthless was his challenge. And there was something else almost mystical to this. His family had made its money on the snowy cotton fibers that had sucked the life out of this land. The multiple textiles that formed the base of the Callaway fortune all came from cotton. Thus, Cason Callaway reasoned, he had an obligation to give back to the country he loved some of the bounty he had received.

With missionary zeal Mr. Callaway not only tackled the land he had acquired but also persuaded business and professional men he knew to buy up one hundred small farms nearby and do the same. They planted pastures and acquired livestock. They sowed grains and planted vineyards and a variety of vegetables. To ensure that his dream continued after him, Mr. Callaway established a foundation named for his mother, Ida Cason Callaway, so that his personal holdings would be preserved and developed "till Gabriel blows his horn."

Wearing worn and earth-stained clothes, topped by an old Panama hat, Cason Callaway walked over his land constantly, talking to workmen and random visitors, seeing the color and shape of the earth in every light. He hired horticulturists for their expertise. One noted expert in wild azaleas, Fred Galle, saw that the flower that started it all, the plumleaf rhododendron, was nurtured, protected, and multiplied exceedingly. Banks of it magically bloomed in the summer, eventually bringing Mr. Callaway a national award from the Garden Club of America for the preservation of this rare and endangered species.

Today, it and other native and cultivated azaleas fill a twenty-acre plot of their own and line a five-mile pathway through the woods.

A visitor once remarked with perhaps a touch of irreverence that Cason Callaway was doing only "what God could do if He had the money." Mr. Callaway's personal goal was that the gardens would look, as much as possible, the way God had made this land before man arrived and began his destruction. He wanted to be a worthy steward of the blessings God had granted him; in a sense, God did have the money, through Cason Callaway.

Wildflowers were a particular hobby of Mrs. Callaway's, and they were first on the list of plants to be saved. Her husband brought in thousands of trees, the native ones first — pines and oaks and hollies and sycamores and beeches — and then the special ones, such as the fragrant tea olive, which he had loved all his life and that he knew could adapt to cultivation.

Magnolias, the stately trees of Old South legend, are native to Georgia, but they had been uprooted and hauled away from the land that was to become Mr. Callaway's garden. Mrs. Callaway lamented their absence when she looked over the Blue Springs garden, and she mentioned to her husband that she would like to have a magnolia.

He went nursery shopping and brought home five thousand seedlings.

Today, the magnificent grandiflora lifts its glistening evergreen foliage and its creamy blossoms of heart-stopping fragrance high in the Callaway forests, along roadways, and in many other Harris County yards as well.

Cason Callaway dreamed it all.

Pleasure garden has its own connotations for children, and for them Mr. Callaway wanted to catch and hold some of the spring water, now miraculously clear, cupping it in lakes and ponds where they could swim and fish with their fathers.

He wanted to cover the baked, cracked earth with lush green grass where people might play golf.

He wanted to see that there were gracefully meandering footpaths moving from deep shade to sunlight for hikers and bicyclists, where in spring they could breathe the fragrance of witch hazel and sweet shrub and tulip poplar and lift their hearts and spirits to a blaze of changing color in autumn.

He built dams that captured water for a chain of thirteen lakes, one of 175 acres and other smaller ones he could skip pebbles across. He hauled in tons of white sand to create the biggest man-made beach in the world. He stocked the lake with the kind of fish he himself, an ardent fisherman, most enjoyed catching. He built a country store for delicacies such as jellies and sauces made from the native muscadine grape. He wanted an inn where visitors might find lodging, rustic cottages where families could reasonably spend weekends or vacations, a restaurant overlooking the lake, and a small, exquisite woodland chapel named for his mother.

Mr. Callaway did not live to see all his dreams come to fruition. In 1961, at sixty-seven, he died. But the vision he passed on is undimmed.

The Ida Cason Callaway Chapel, built of fieldstone and arched timbers from the nearby hills, stands beside a natural waterfall at the head of a small lake. It is the sanctuary for meditation and worship that Cason Callaway foresaw, and it has also become the chosen site for the weddings of scores of young couples setting out to pursue their own dreams. Every Sunday throughout the year, an organ concert fills the chapel with the sounds of worship, but on most days the tranquil quiet is unbroken except for birdsong and the occasional flash of a frog or a fish in the waters of the lake.

Once Cason Callaway wistfully remarked that he wished all children could have beauty in their lives, true beauty, not transitory flash or glamour. He meant the beauty that comes with learning, from seeing birds and flowers and fish and even lowly

skunks and box turtles and truly knowing about them. That wish, too, has come true in the splendid John A. Sibley Horticultural Center, which opened in 1984. The Sibley Center is the heart of a teaching program for thousands of people, young and old, who attend classes year-round. The award-winning Sibley Conservatory, one of the handsomest in the nation, provides climate control for the cultivation of spectacular flower displays deployed around a two-story waterfall.

A dazzling new reality in the world of Cason Callaway's dream is the Day Butterfly Center, which opened in 1988. Here, thousands of butterflies, both native and imported, live out their life cycles, feasting on flowers planted for their pleasure. The Day Center, the largest free-flight, glass-enclosed conservatory in North America, was inspired by a gift from Mrs. Deen Day Smith of the Days Inn family; thus, another part of Mr. Callaway's dream continues, as other philanthropists join the effort he began.

Students and photographers of these "air-borne flowers" spend hours in the seven-thousand-square-foot conservatory observing the birth and life cycles of the butterflies. To foster the education of gardeners, the center has a series of outdoor wildlife gardens to show how a home garden can feature plants that will attract butterflies.

"Mr. Cason's vegetable garden," the affectionate name used by the staff, is a spot to which the founder of the gardens would have come again and again because it combines the elements he most valued in a pleasure garden. It is beautiful with flowers and herbs and plants that attract butterflies, but it is also seven sumptuous acres of food for the table, grown on soil that once was believed to be too dispirited to produce.

Public television's *Victory Garden* bases its southern segments in "Mr. Cason's vegetable garden," showing the world what can be done with the land and the seasons and skills that Mr. Cason wanted to teach all lovers of the earth.

Through this exposure and other similar attention and through the thousands of visitors who enjoy the special Callaway brand of hospitality each year, Mr. Cason's personal dream and his generous vision now reach far beyond the boundaries of the pleasure garden he carved out of the Depression soil of south Georgia in the same way a sculptor releases the angel hidden within the block of marble.

Cason Callaway's gardens are concrete evidence that a blessed man can return very special thanks by setting the most glorious table imaginable and inviting the world to partake forever in his dream.

— Celestine Sibley
Fall 1988

CALLAWAY
GARDENS

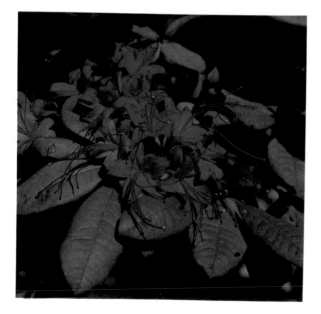

*The
Cecil B. Day
Butterfly
Center*

The John A. Sibley Horticultural Center

The Gardens Restaurant

The Country Store

Pioneer Log Cabin

Information Center

The Gardens Restaurant

The Country Store

Pioneer Log Cabin

Information Center

Mr. Cason's Vegetable Garden

"Victory Garden South"